Cracking the Code

James Driver

PACIFIC
LEARNING

© 2004 **Pacific Learning**
© 2002 Written by **James Driver**
Photography: title page and p. 14 Ancient Art & Architecture; p. 4 Ancient Art & Architecture; p. 6 Science & Society Picture Library; p. 7 Science & Society Picture Library (all); p. 12 Corbis UK (top), Ancient Art & Architecture (bottom left & right); p. 15 British Museum; pp. 16, 17 Ancient Art & Architecture; p. 18 Mary Evans Picture Library (top), Oxford Scientific Films/Maurice Tibbles (bottom); p. 19 Mary Evans Picture Library; p. 20 Science Photo Library (top), Telegraph Colour Library (bottom); p. 21 SPL (top), Corbis UK (bottom); p. 22 Tropix (left), RNIB, Peterborough (bottom); p. 23 S. & R. Greenhill; p. 24 National Gallery; p. 25 Ancient Art & Architecture (top right), OSF/G. MacLean (left), OSF/T. Heathcote (bottom); p. 26 Map reproduced from Ordance Survey Landranger mapping with the permission of the Controller of Her Majesty's Stationery Office. ©Crown copyright. Licence no. 100000249. Cover Photograph by Science & Society Picture Library; back Cover by Ancient Art & Architecture
Illustrated by Martin Aston, Stefan Chabluk, and Martin McKenna
U.S. edit by **Alison Auch**

With many thanks to Dr. Paul Stephens and Alex Dumestre for their expert and patient assistance.

This Americanized Edition of *Cracking the Code,* originally published in England in 2002, is published by arrangement with Oxford University Press.

08 07 06 05 04
10 9 8 7 6 5 4 3 2 1

Published by
Pacific Learning
P.O. Box 2723
Huntington Beach, CA 92647-0723
www.pacificlearning.com

ISBN: 1-59055-437-X
PL-7522

Printed in China.

CONTENTS

WHAT IS A CODE?

If you can see and hear someone, it is very easy to send that person a message. As long as you both speak the same language, you can talk to each other, shout at each other, or whisper secretly.

If you can see, but cannot hear each other, you can still communicate by making signals with your hands.

You can ask someone to come toward you.

You can ask someone to stop.

However, if you cannot see or hear the other person, or if you want your message to be a secret that no one else can understand, you will have to send it in a different way. You might use a code.

▲ Julius Caesar (102–44 BC)

Secret Codes

Julius Caesar, the famous Roman general, often sent messages that he did not want his enemies to read. To ensure secrecy, he used a very simple code.

The Roman **alphabet** had only twenty-three letters, but when Caesar wanted to send a confidential message, he did not spell words with the usual letters, he counted three letters ahead and used those letters instead. So in a coded message, his name CAESAR would be FDHXDV.

▲ The Romans did not have the letters "J," "U," or

4

DIFFERENT TYPES OF CODE

Not all codes are secret. In fact, many have been used by millions of people.

Writing

Writing is a code. If you are writing in English, you use the twenty-six letters in the alphabet. The letters often stand for the sounds you make when you speak.

There are lots of different systems of writing, and they all use different codes. The ancient Egyptians wrote with pictures, called **hieroglyphics**, instead of letters. They wrote "water" like this:

The ancient Sumerians started writing with picture shapes too, but these gradually evolved into a set of signs called **cuneiform**. The Sumerians wrote "water" like this:

FACT BOX

What Is a Code?
A code is a way of passing ideas or information on to other people. A code only works if the person who sends the message and the person who receives the message both understand how the code works.

Semaphore

Before the invention of radio communication, sailors used to send messages from one ship to another by using **semaphore**. By holding two flags in different positions, they could spell out all the letters of the alphabet.

This is what the word "water" looks like when it is sent by semaphore:

See page 10

Morse Code

Some codes use sounds. The most famous of these is **Morse code**, which uses two sounds: a short buzz, which is called a "dot," and a long buzz, which is called a "dash."

Anyone using Morse code has to learn how the dots and dashes are used to represent the different letters of the alphabet.

See page 19

When "water" is written in **Morse code**, it looks like this:

CODING MACHINES

In 1918, a German engineer named Arthur Scherbius created what many people thought was the perfect coding machine. He gave it an ancient Greek name – Enigma – meaning "secret" or "mystery."

Enigma operators were directed to follow these instructions:

1. You, and the person receiving the message, must decide which three letter rotors you are going to use today. (There are five to choose from. Each one has the alphabet on it in a different order.)

2. Agree on the order the rotors are going to be placed in the machine.

3. Decide which electrical circuits you are going to use. (You make a circuit by plugging short cables into the sockets on the plugboard. The circuits light up the lights on the panel.)

4. Start typing your message on the keyboard.

5. Typing a letter on the keyboard makes a light come on by a different letter on the lightboard. That is the coded letter for today.

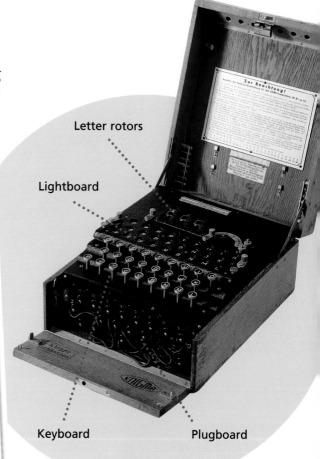

Letter rotors

Lightboard

Keyboard

Plugboard

▲ An Enigma coding machine

FACT BOX

Being able to choose different letter rotors, different alphabet orders, and different circuits meant that Enigma had an astounding 150,000,000,000,000 different starting positions!

CODE-BREAKING MACHINES

nigma's incredible number of starting
ositions meant that the code could be
hanged every day.

Some Enigma machines held an extra letter
rotor. This made it even harder to crack the
coded messages!

Alan Turing

British mathematician Alan Turing
realized that the best way to beat one
ingenious machine was to build another,
more ingenious machine.

Turing had not enjoyed school, but
he was fascinated by math, which he
studied at Cambridge University in
England. When war broke out between
Britain and Germany in 1939, he was
summoned to Bletchley Park in England,
the secret base for code breakers.

With the help of Gordon Welchman,
Turing designed the Turing Bombe.
This huge machine could test the
different choices the Enigma operators
might have made that day. Their early
computer helped the British crack
the Enigma code and uncover most of
the German's secret plans, which
resulted in many lives being saved.

Colossus

Two years later, the Germans changed
the way they used their codes. A bigger,
faster decoding machine was needed. In
1943, the first programmable electronic
computer, called Colossus, came into use
as a code breaker.

◀ Colossus was designed by Tommy Flowers,
a Post Office engineer.

MAKING YOUR OWN CODE

STEP 1 Choose a key phrase.

strangers on a desert island

STEP 2 Take out all the letters that appear twice. Write down the letters that remain.

strangeodil

STEP 3 Now, write down the rest of the alphabet, but do not use any letter that has already appeared in your key phrase.

strangeodilbcfhjkmpquvwxyz

STEP 4 Confirm that you have twenty-six letters!

STEP 5 Write the alphabet beneath your code.

s	t	r	a	n	g	e	o	d	i	l	b	c	f	h	j	k	m	p	q	u	v	w	x	y	z
a	b	c	d	e	f	g	h	i	j	k	l	m	n	o	p	q	r	s	t	u	v	w	x	y	z

STEP 6 Write out the message you want to send.

see you in the library

STEP 7 To turn the message into code, find each letter in the bottom line and replace it with the letter in the line above.

pnn yhu df qon bdtmsmy

STEP 8 If someone sends you a message in code that is based on the same key phrase, you can read it by finding the letter in the top line and replacing it with the corresponding letter from the line below.

fdrn iht!

THE DANCING MEN

To find out more about this code, you will have to read Sir Arthur Conan Doyle's "Adventure of the Dancing Men" in *The Return of Sherlock Holmes*.

British author Sir Arthur Conan Doyle (1859–1930) made his great detective character, Sherlock Holmes, solve one very difficult case by cracking a code that looked like a line of dancing figures.

Sherlock Holmes was Sir Arthur Conan Doyle's most famous fictional character.

Holmes starts with the vital piece of knowledge that the most frequently used letters in the English language are:

e t a o i n s h r d l u

So he assumes the figure that appears most often could be the letter "e."

For a while he is puzzled that some of the figures in the longer messages carry flags.

Then he realizes that these might not be letters, but simply show the gaps between words.
Next he looks for words that use "e" more than once. As the name of the woman who is receiving the coded messages is "Elsie," he guesses that this is her name:

That gives him "l," "s," and "i."

Reading as "never"

gives him three more letters: "n," "v," and "r." His solution is almost complete!

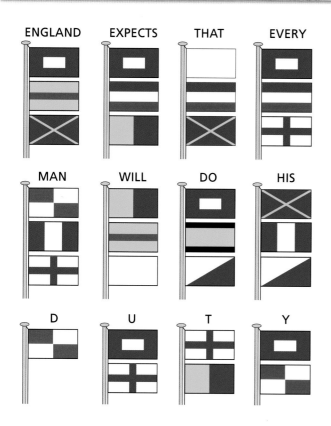

ENGLAND EXPECTS THAT EVERY

MAN WILL DO HIS

D U T Y

On October 21, 1805, the most famous signal in naval history was flown during the **Battle of Trafalgar** from the rigging of HMS *Victory* – the flagship of Admiral Horatio Nelson. It was made up of thirty-one flags.

Nelson was going to use the word "confides," but the officer in charge of signaling, Flag Lieutenant John Pasco, pointed out that "expects" was already in the naval code book and could be sent using only three flags. "Confides," like the word "duty," would have to be spelled out letter by letter.

Semaphore

Semaphore also uses flags to send messages. Yet unlike a flag code in which different combinations of flags represent different words and letters, semaphore relies on the person sending the message to spell out each word by holding the flags in different positions for each individual letter.

A B C D E F G

H I J K L M N

O P Q R S T U

V W X Y Z

ERALDRY

attles in the Middle Ages were often
onfused, brutal events, with soldiers
sing swords, daggers, axes, and clubs
o attack their enemies.

Unfortunately, it was all too easy to
nistake a friend for an enemy.

To help knights identify each other,
n peace and in war, an elaborate code
f **heraldry** was developed. No words
vere involved. Heraldry used patterns,
ymbols, and colors.

Like many codes, heraldry developed
n elaborate **jargon** of its own and
eeded specialists, the Heralds of
he College of Arms, to ensure that
veryone followed the rules.

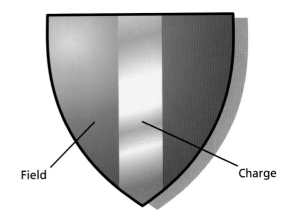

Field _____ Charge

▲ To describe a heraldic device you
name the **field** first, then the **charge**.
So this shield is "azure, a pale or."

A Knight's Shield

The surface of the shield is the field.
Anything placed on the field is called a
charge. The simplest charges were
called **ordinaries**.

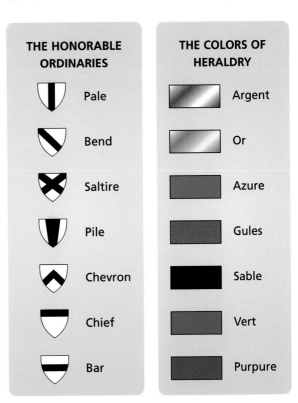

THE HONORABLE ORDINARIES		THE COLORS OF HERALDRY	
	Pale		Argent
	Bend		Or
	Saltire		Azure
	Pile		Gules
	Chevron		Sable
	Chief		Vert
	Bar		Purpure

WRITING CODES: PICTOGRAPHS TO PHONOGRAMS

If you can write, you can record what you observe and how you feel. Your original ideas and deepest thoughts can be kept safe, and, if you wish, passed on for other people to read.

Writing allows you to invent imaginative worlds and to fill them with people, places, and events that can be enjoyed by anyone who has cracked the code by learning to read.

For more than 20,000 years, humans have painted pictures, carved sculptures in stone, sung songs, and told stories to communicate. They only began writing about 5,000 years ago.

The Long Room in the Old Library at Trinity College, Dublin, contains more than 200,000 books.

▲ Cuneiform writing on a clay tablet from about 3000 BC

▼ Hunting scene in a cave painting

The first writing was used solely for record keeping. Shapes were impressed on wet clay with a pointed stick or reed. When the clay hardened in the sun, it could be stored away safely as a permanent record.

Phonograms

In about 2800 BC, the symbols the scribes were using for individual words began to be used for the *sounds* people made when they spoke that word. This was the most important step in the entire history of writing.

The Sumerian word for "ox" was "gu," so whenever another word contained the "gu" sound, the scribe could use the ox symbol to show the reader that was the way to pronounce that portion of the word. A sound symbol that helps to make a new word is called a **phonogram**.

ictographs

he very earliest records used were **ictographs**. If oxen were being ecorded, the **scribes** drew a little icture of an ox's head. People soon ound it quicker to turn the picture into shape that was simpler to draw and hat all the other scribes would use and ecognize.

This early, wedge-shaped style of riting is called cuneiform.

◀ Picture of an ox's head

◀ Cuneiform symbol for an ox's head

Egyptian Hieroglyphics

The same system was used in ancient Egypt. The ancient Egyptians' use of symbols as both pictograms and phonograms was called hieroglyphics. The Egyptians took the strongest sound from a word and used the pictograph of that word as the phonogram.

Pictograph		Phonogram sound
(mouth symbol)	mouth	r
(house symbol)	house	pr
(face symbol)	face	hr

The Sumerians needed hundreds of phonograms because their language, like every spoken language in the world, had a huge number of possible sounds: "ba," "be," "bi," "bo," "bu," and so on.

However, the alphabet with which we are familiar has only twenty-six letters.

a b c d e f g h i j k l m n o p q r s t u v w x y z

In about 1800 BC, someone, probably living near the coast of Palestine, had the idea that the simplest way to organize writing was to give each major sound its own letter.

We will probably never determine who invented the first alphabet, althoug the ancient Greeks said it was Cadmus who brought them their alphabet. Still, we can figure out a likely scenario.

Inventing the Alphabet

1. The inventor looked at the pictographs of a word in a language we now call West Semitic.

2. That pictograph was used as a letter to represent the very first sound in that word.

Pictograph	Pronunciation	First sound
∿∿∿	mayyuma	*m*
✝	tawwu	*t*

Not all the pictographs matched the letter of our modern alphabet so closel

Pictograph	Pronunciation	First sound
‿‿	kappu	*k*
♀	wawwu	*w*

◀ The Sphinx in Egypt, with letters from an early alphabet carved on its base

An inscription in ancient Greek, from the city of Thessaloniki

Another major difference is that vowels ("a," "e," "i," "o," "u") did not appear in the earliest alphabets.

Rdng ths wtht vwls shld nt b tht hrd!

The first alphabet with vowels was the one used by the ancient Greeks. Although it is possible to read and write without them, with a language such as ancient Greek or modern English, in which many words *begin* with vowels, it becomes much more difficult.

How the Alphabet Spread

The Greeks based their alphabet on the one used by the merchants who came to trade with them from the coast of **Phoenicia**. When the Greeks reached Italy, they passed their version on to the Etruscans, who were then conquered by the Romans, who in turn went on to conquer much of the rest of Europe. Explorers from Europe then ferried the alphabet to other parts of the world, such as North and South America and Australia.

THE ROSETTA STONE

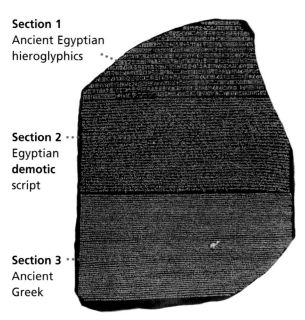

Section 1
Ancient Egyptian
hieroglyphics

Section 2
Egyptian
demotic
script

Section 3
Ancient
Greek

▲ The Rosetta Stone, now in the British Museum, London

The Rosetta Stone was discovered in 1799. It supplied written information in three different forms: ancient Egyptian hieroglyphics, later Egyptian demotic script, and ancient Greek.

When the stone was found, nobody knew how to read hieroglyphics. There was some understanding of demotic, but every one of the ancient Greek words could be translated.

The French scholar Jean-Francois Champollion (1790–1832) realized that if he could match a known Greek word with an unknown hieroglyph, he might be able to crack the long-forgotten code of ancient Egypt.

He started with the **cartouche** – a set of hieroglyphs put inside a long oval box. After studying the Greek section, Champollion decided this must be the name "Ptolemy." He compared it with cartouche from another Egyptian inscription, thought to be the name "Cleopatra."

The first symbol in "Ptolemy" and the fifth in "Cleopatra" were the same. The fourth in "Ptolemy" and the second in "Cleopatra" were the same. Champollion figured out that the first letter in the "Cleopatra" cartouche was "K" (Kleopatra is the Greek version of her name), and that the bird hieroglyph must represent "a."

Champollion had found his way into the code!

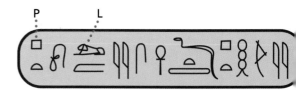

P   L

▲ The Egyptian name "Ptolemy," featured on the Rosetta Stone

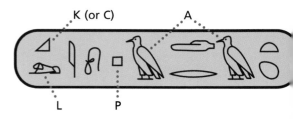

K (or C)   A

L   P

▲ The Egyptian name "Cleopatra"

ᚠᚢᚦᚨᚱᚲᚺᚾᛁᛊᛏᛒᛗᛚ

The angular shape of **runes** meant they could be easily carved in stone, antler, wood, ivory, or other hard materials. Runic alphabets were used in northern Europe from about AD 200 to 900. The early alphabets had twenty-four letters. Then around AD 800, the Vikings developed one with only sixteen letters.

▼ The Franks Casket dates from the 8th century AD. It is carved from whalebone.

The runes on the Franks Casket are not actually related to the story shown in the carvings. Instead, they spell out a short poem about a whale being stranded and dying on a beach.

Secret runes, for casting spells, cursing an enemy, or bestowing special powers upon a weapon, were often made by adding or taking away some of the usual lines so that only the person writing knew what was being said.

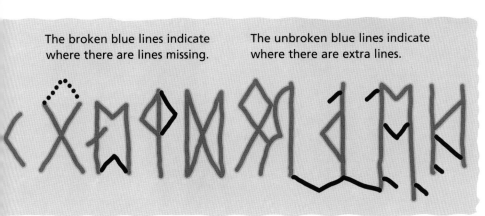

The broken blue lines indicate where there are lines missing.

The unbroken blue lines indicate where there are extra lines.

◀ These magic runes were carved on an ancient tomb in Norway. They admonish the living to keep away!

INTERNATIONAL LANGUAGES

Esperanto

In 1887, a Polish doctor, Dr L. L. Zamenhof, invented a language that could be used throughout the entire world. He based his language mainly on the words and grammar used in Latin and French, but he also included ideas from German, English, Russian, Polish, and Greek.

Zamenhof wanted his language – now known as **Esperanto** – to be a code that everyone could share. He thought that when two people met it would be more fair if they spoke a language that they had both had to learn, rather than one of them having the advantage of speaking it from birth.

Dr. Zamenhof called himself ▶ "Dr. Esperanto."

Latin

▲ The Brown trout – *Salmo trutta*

Hungarians call a trout *pisztrang*, Spaniards call it *trucha,* and the Dutch call it *forel*. Yet when biologists in these and other countries write about trout they all use the same Latin name – *Salmo trutta*. Latin is an ancient language utilized by Western scholars for hundreds of years.

FACT BOX

American English
The Internet was developed in the United States, so much of the information on it is written in American English. Because the Internet can be accessed from anywhere in the world, many people think that American English will become the first truly international language.

MORSE CODE

The American painter and inventor Samuel Morse (1791–1872) designed his innovative code to work on his **electric telegraph**. To operate the telegraph, an electric current was passed along miles of wire. By pressing and releasing the handle of the telegraph key, the electric circuit along these wires could be completed or broken.

Holding the key down for a short time produced a short buzz – a dot; holding it a long time made a dash. Morse's code put dots and dashes together to make the letters of the alphabet.

An Italian, Guglielmo Marconi, invented a way of transmitting sound without wires – wireless telegraphy. In 1901, he used Morse code to transmit a message 2,000 miles (3,218 km) across the Atlantic.

Morse Code

A ·_	H ····	O _ _ _	V ···_
B _···	I ··	P ·_ _·	W ·_ _
C _·_·	J ·_ _ _	Q _ _·_	X _··_
D _··	K _·_	R ·_·	Y _·_ _
E ·	L ·_··	S ···	Z _ _··
F ··_·	M _ _	T _	
G _ _·	N _·	U ··_	

1 ·_ _ _ _   2 ··_ _ _   3 ···_ _   4 ····_   5 ·····
6 _····   7 _ _···   8 _ _ _··   9 _ _ _ _·   0 _ _ _ _ _

In 1912, when the *Titanic* hit an iceberg and began to sink, one of the wireless operators, John Phillips, stayed at his post sending messages for help. His Morse code messages were heard on a ship called the *Carpathia*.

◄ The *Titanic* sank before the *Carpathia* came to its rescue. John Phillips froze to death in the frigid water.

DNA: THE CODE FOR LIFE

All plants and animals contain a substance called **DNA**. It is made up of four chemicals, or bases: guanine (G), adenine (A), thymine (T), and cytosine (C). These bases can be linked together in different ways, and these patterns, or codes, generate the differences in the way we look and act.

Almost every cell in your body contains three billion bases! The bases in the DNA are grouped together to make **genes**. There are about 100,000 genes in each cell.

Each gene makes a different protein. Proteins get things done – they give color to our eyes, make our muscles move, and digest our food.

Everyone's DNA is slightly different. It is a mixture of both parents' DNA. Because the code of everyone's genes is slightly different, we are all unique in looks and behavior.

▼ The four bases pair up to make what look like the rungs on a twisted ladder. This shape is called a double helix.

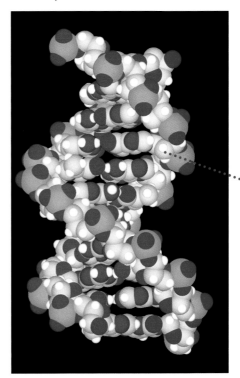

bases in pairs

FACT BOX

Because everyone's DNA is a little bit different, detectives always search the scene of a crime very carefully. If they find a speck of blood, or even a single hair, they can check if its DNA matches the DNA of the person they suspect.

▲ We inherit our genes from our biological parents, but everyone looks slightly different.

BINARY:
THE CODE OF THE COMPUTER

Many **number** systems use ten digits – probably because most of us have hands with a total of ten fingers and thumbs! Computers do not have fingers and thumbs, but they do have millions of **transistors**. A transistor can either be on or off. By writing precise instructions that stop and start the electrical current passing through the transistors, a computer programmer can make a computer store and process data.

▲ The calculating machines and early computers, used before electronic computers, were very large.

To instruct the computer, the programmer uses a simple, but very powerful number system, called the **binary code**. The binary code uses only two digits: 0 and 1. When the transistor reads 0 it switches off; when it reads 1 it switches on.

Using only two digits keeps the entire process simple. This means that the transistors are easy to make, cheap, reliable, and can be built very small.

▲ A twenty-first century handheld notebook: as technology advances, computers are getting smaller and smaller.

THE BRAILLE ALPHABET

The braille alphabet is used by people who are blind or visually impaired.

▲ People read braille by running their fingertips over a series of dots that are raised up from the surface of the page.

Braille was developed by a Frenchman, Louis Braille (1809–1852), who was blinded after an accident in his father's workshop at the age of three.

The basic building block of braille is the six-dot cell, arranged and numbered like this:

1	● ●	4
2	● ●	5
3	● ●	6

Various combinations of the six dots make the alphabet. They also stand for common words, such as "and," "for," "the," and "with"; common parts of words such as "ch," "gh," "sh," "ed," an "ing"; punctuation marks; and signs to show capital letters, accents, and number

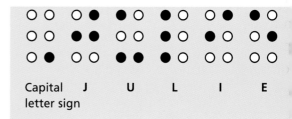

Capital J   U   L   I   E
letter sign

Braille books are meticulously proofread by blind people who, while listening to audiotapes of the text, check the braille version with their fingers.

▲ Braille pages are printed by punching the raised dots on paper running over metal printing plates that have the pattern of raised dots molded on them.

SIGNING

▲ These girls are using signing to help them communicate

For hundreds of years, people who are deaf or hearing impaired have communicated by using hands, fingers, facial expressions, and overall body language. There are **signing** alphabets, so individual words can be spelled out – but far more common is the use of gestures to represent whole words.

Sign languages are not international. Just as spoken languages differ across the world, so do sign languages. What surprises many people is that countries that have very similar spoken languages, such as Britain and the United States, have completely separate sign languages.

One of the primary differences between American Sign Language (ASL) and British Sign Language (BSL) is that you use only one hand to sign the ASL alphabet, but people use two hands to spell out letters in BSL.

▼ The ASL signs for the alphabet (top), and a message in BSL (bottom).

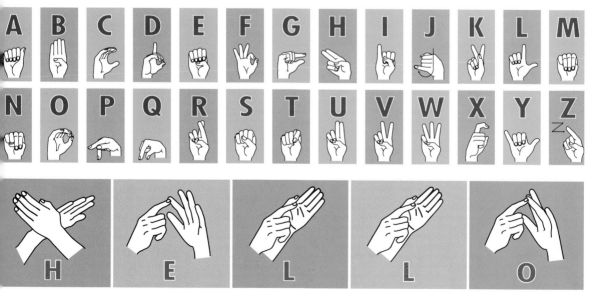

SYMBOLS IN ART

Hans Holbein (1497–1543) painted this portrait of two Frenchmen who visited the English king, Henry VIII, in 1533, when the two countries were arguing over religion. The French wanted England to remain a Catholic country, but King Henry broke away from the Catholic Church. This dispute eventually led to England becoming a Protestant country.

Holbein added symbols to help anyone looking at the picture understand the controversy.

This sundial shows two different times! Holbein wanted to illustrate how the quarrel had disturbed what everyone had always agreed on in the past.

A string on this lute is broken and needs to be repaired. Holbein was hoping that the two countries would mend the rift that was keeping them from working together.

This is a Protestant hymnbook, but it is open so it looks like the two French Catholic men have been using it. Holbein is showing that it is possible for both religions to share the same ideas.

This is a skull! Look at it from the right-hand edge of the page. It is a symbol of death. Holbein is warning that life is too short to argue.

During the Middle Ages, most people living in Europe believed that the plants and animals they encountered every day were exactly the same as the first plants and animals God made for Adam and Eve. They also believed that God had left them clues as to how they could use these plants. His code was called the Doctrine of Signatures.

▲ This stained glass window from a church shows Adam and Eve in the Garden of Eden.

Hound's-tongue

Because the plant called hound's-tongue has leaves that look and feel like the tongue of a dog, it was believed that if a person were bitten by a dog, putting these leaves on the wound would heal it.

Eyebright

The brilliantly colored flowers of eyebright are so bright that people believed the plant could be made into a potion that would cure bad eyesight.

25

MAPS

Mapmakers turn three-dimensional objects, such as mountains, rivers, roads, forests, railroads, highways, cities, towns, and lakes, into an easy-to-use two-dimensional format. Maps show us what is out of sight, what is hidden away, and help us to find our way to where we want to go.

To read a map you need to know the code. To help you crack the code, mapmakers usually include a helpful **key**.

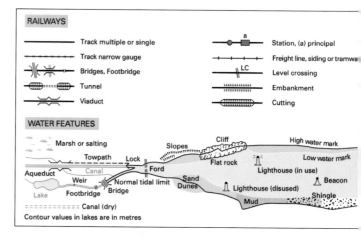

▲ Part of the standard Ordnance Survey key, used in Britain, showing railroads and water features.

The symbols that make up the keys on these two maps are often used in British maps. Once you understand the symbols for a map from anywhere in the world, you can plan a journey.

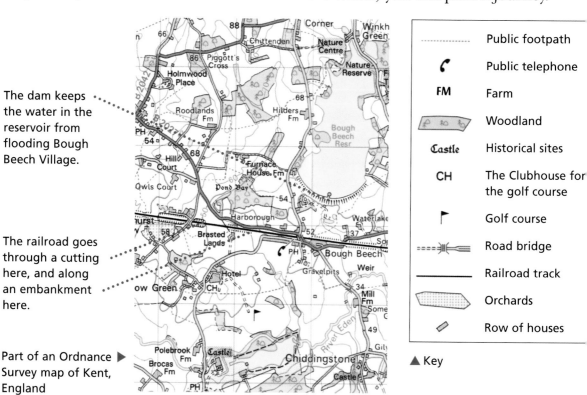

The dam keeps the water in the reservoir from flooding Bough Beech Village.

The railroad goes through a cutting here, and along an embankment here.

Part of an Ordnance ▶ Survey map of Kent, England

▲ Key

SLANG

Slang is one of the most daunting codes to crack. One week a word is trendy, the next week anyone using it is laughed at for being out-of-date.

Lots of different groups of people use slang. Australian children might "dob" in their "mates." Computer users discuss "flamers" and "surfing the net." Soccer players "nutmeg" opponents when they fool them by passing the ball between their legs.

"Surfing the net"

"Nutmeg"

Mall Cutpurse was a well-known thief in London in the seventeenth century. She disguised herself as a man.

In the seventeenth century, slang was used by criminals to disguise what they were talking about. Thieves' slang was called "cant."

"*Bring a waste*, you *prigger of prancers! If we don't budge a beak* the only *cony-catching* we'll do will be in the *counter*."

If you crack the "cant" code, this means:

"*Get out of here*, you *horse thief! If we don't escape from the police* the only *crimes* we'll do will be in *prison*."

BODY LANGUAGE

Humans are the only members of the animal kingdom who have developed the extraordinary code of speech. There are more than six billion people in the world, and more than 5,000 languages are spoken.

In Roman times, this hand ▶ gesture was used by spectators watching gladiators fighting to decide whether the gladiator would live or die.

In addition to speech, we use another code that many scientists believe was used by our ancestors long before they developed the power of speech.

▼ This gesture means "quiet."

▼ It is easy to guess how this man feels!

"Ssshhh!"

▼ This gesture uses the face, hands, and shoulders to send the message:

By using signs and gestures, by moving and positioning our hands, eyes, eyebrows, lips, arms, legs, shoulders – practically every part of our body – we send explicit messages that tell anyone watching us how and what we are feeling. This code is called nonverbal communication (NVC).

"I don't know

FIRE, SMOKE, AND SOUND

Messages without Words

BEACON CHAINS

What? A line of bonfires

Why? To warn of invasion

How? If enemies appear, light a beacon. Smoke or flames are seen by the next community who in turn light their beacon, and the warning spreads across the country.

Where and when? Southern England, 1588, for the Spanish Armada. Hadrian's Wall, AD 120–440

SMOKE SIGNALS

What? A fire of grass and leaves

Why? To send simple messages across open country

How? Light a large fire and feed with damp grass or green leaves to produce a huge plume of smoke. Soak a blanket in water. Cover the fire to trap the smoke. Whip away the blanket. A huge puff of smoke rises into the sky.

Where and when? North American plains, nineteenth century

WHISTLES

What? Lips; wooden, metal, and plastic tubes

Why? To send simple instructions

How? Long, short, high-pitched, low-pitched blasts. Can all have different meanings, for instance, "stop," "sit," "stay," "go."

Where and when? Herders, animal trainers, referees and umpires, lifeguards.

NUMBERS

Thousands of years ago, **nomadic** people lived by hunting and gathering. No one used numbers because no one really needed them. Nomadic people simply talked in quantities: "There is plenty of water, we'll stay here." "There are not enough kangaroos here, we should move on."

As people began to settle in permanent places, they needed to keep track of many things, such as animals and crops. Counting, weighing, and measuring became important.

People in different places developed different number systems. Our modern arabic number system is actually believed to have been created in India. From there, it was transmitted to the Arabs, who developed it further and carried it to Europe. By 1300, the arabic system was used throughout Europe.

▼ For hundreds of years, farmers have used rhym to keep a verbal record of the number of animals in their flocks and herds. This one was still being used in the Lake District in England less than fifty years ago!

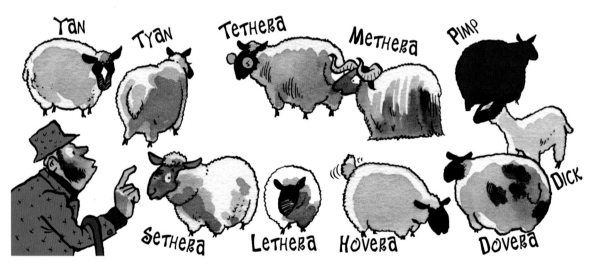

YAN TYAN TETHERA METHERA PIMP SETHERA LETHERA HOVERA DOVERA DICK

Number Systems

	Modern arabic									
Modern arabic	1	2	3	4	5	6	7	8	9	10
Early arabic	1	2	3	ع	٩	6	7	8	9	0
Roman	I	II	III	IV	V	VI	VII	VIII	IX	X
Mayan	o	oo	ooo	oooo	—	ō	ō̄	ō̄̄	ō̄̄̄	=

GLOSSARY

phabet – a set of letters that represent sounds

ttle of Trafalgar – famous naval battle in which a British fleet defeated Spanish and French fleets

nary code – a number code that uses only two digits – 0 and 1

rtouche – a set of hieroglyphs, usually representing an important name, surrounded by an unbroken oval line

arge – a design painted on a knight's shield

neiform – a style of early writing that used simple, wedge-shaped lines

motic – a style of writing that simplified the hieroglyphic system used in ancient Egypt

NA – the substance that carries the code that determines what individual living things will look like

ectric telegraph – a machine that sends messages along a wire by completing or breaking an electrical circuit

speranto – an artificial international language

eld – the surface color of a knight's shield

ne – a vital part of the DNA code

raldry – a code used by knights in the Middle Ages to identify each other without using words

eroglyphic – a system of writing based on pictures

rgon – special words used by a group of people, such as scientists

key – the part of a map that explains all the different symbols

Morse code – a code that represents the letters of the alphabet through short and long bursts of sound or light

nomadic – a lifestyle in which people move around without settling in one place

number – a symbol that represents individual, or groups of, objects

ordinaries – simple shapes used in heraldry

Phoenicia – an area that is now the coastal region of Syria, Lebanon, and Israel

phonogram – a shape used to represent a sound in early writing

pictograph – a picture used to represent a word in early writing

rune – a letter used in early northern European writing

scribe – a person who writes down what someone else says

semaphore – a code that represents the letters of the alphabet through flags held in different positions

signing – a way of communicating used by people who are deaf or hearing impaired

slang – an informal code used by groups of people who invent words to describe things that are a big part of their lives

symbol – a sign or a shape that stands for something else

transistor – a tiny electronic device that controls the flow of electricity

INDEX